AMAZING MILITARY MACHINES

AIRCRAFT CARRIERS

BY ELEAN

Enslow PUBLISHING

Please visit our website, www.enslow.com. For a free color catalog of all our high-quality books, call toll free 1-800-398-2504 or fax 1-877-980-4454.

Library of Congress Cataloging-in-Publication Data
Names: Bradshaw, Eleanor, author.
Title: Aircraft carriers / Eleanor Bradshaw.
Description: Buffalo, New York : Enslow Publishing, 2025. | Series: Amazing military machines | Includes index.
Identifiers: LCCN 2023058684 | ISBN 9781978539532 (library binding) | ISBN 9781978539525 (paperback) | ISBN 9781978539549 (ebook)
Subjects: LCSH: Aircraft carriers–United States–Juvenile literature.
Classification: LCC V874.3 .B727 2025 | DDC 623.825/50973–dc23/eng/20240131
LC record available at https://lccn.loc.gov/2023058684

Published in 2025 by
Enslow Publishing
2544 Clinton Street
Buffalo, NY 14224

Portions of this work were originally authored by Ryan Nagelhout and published as *Aircraft Carriers*. All new material in this edition is authored by Eleanor Bradshaw.

Designer: Andrea Davison-Bartolotta
Editor: Rachael Morlock

Photo credits: Cover Aditya0635/Shutterstock.com; series art (metal background texture) caesart/Shutterstock.com; series art (title font) TortugaStudios/Shutterstock.com; p. 5 apiguide/Shutterstock.com; p. 7 U.S. Navy photo by Mass Communication Specialist Seaman Nicholas A. Groesch/Wikimedia Images; p. 9 U.S. Navy photo by Mass Communication Specialist 2nd Class Brian Morales/Released/Flickr; p. 10 U.S. Navy photo by Mass Communication Specialist Seaman Apprentice Ryan J. Mayes/Released/Flickr; p. 11 Greg Meland/Shutterstock.com; p. 13 (bottom) U.S. Navy photo by Mass Communication Specialist 3rd Class Jeffry A. Willadsen/Released/Wikimedia Images; p. 13 (top) U.S. Navy photo by Mass Communication Specialist 2nd Class Alex King/Released/Flickr; p. 15 courtesy of Library of Congress; p. 17 (inset) U.S. Navy Naval Aviation News January 1962/Wikimedia Images; p. 17 (main) Everett Collection/Shutterstock.com; p. 19 steve estvanik/Shutterstock.com; p. 20 U.S. Navy photo by Ricky Thompson/Released/Flickr; p. 21 Aerial-motion/Shutterstock.com.

Printed in the United States of America

CPSIA compliance information: Batch #CS25ENS: For further information contact Enslow Publishing, at 1-800-398-2504.

CONTENTS

Boldface words appear in Words to Know.

FLOATING RUNWAYS

An aircraft carrier is a large **military** ship that carries airplanes, jets, or helicopters. The ship gives these aircraft a place to land and take off at sea. Aircraft carriers sail all over the world, in times of war or peace.

Aircraft carriers are the biggest military ships. They are more than 1,000 feet (305 m) long!

NAVY SHIPS

Aircraft carriers are used by a navy. A navy is the part of a military that works at sea. Many countries have at least one aircraft carrier in their navy. Carriers bring aircraft closer to battles. They also **deliver** supplies and patrol the seas.

Aircraft carriers can be used to deliver food and water to people after a bad storm or other **emergency**.

SHIP AND CREW

Aircraft carriers have many levels and tons of parts. Lots of different people and machines work together on the carrier. They keep the ship working and help the aircraft fly safely. The flight deck is where aircraft take off and land.

Crew members on the flight deck use hand **signals** to tell the **pilots** where to go.

ON THE FLIGHT DECK

Planes don't have much room to take off or land on a carrier. A **catapult** helps planes take off faster. For landing, planes might use a **tailhook** to help them stop. The hook catches onto strong cables on the deck.

The command center of an aircraft carrier is called the island. It is very tall and looks over the flight deck.

CITY AT SEA

A lot happens below the flight deck of an aircraft carrier. As many as 5,000 people can live and work on board. An aircraft carrier has its own hospital, barbershop, and post office! It can stay at sea for many months.

Some of the **sailors** on an aircraft carrier are cooks who make meals for the whole crew.

FIRST AIRCRAFT CARRIERS

Before there were aircraft carriers, a pilot named Eugene Ely learned how to take off and land on other warships. In 1910, Ely took off from the USS *Birmingham*. Landing was harder. In 1911, Ely made his first landing on the USS *Pennsylvania*.

Eugene Ely taught himself how to fly in 1910.

The USS *Langley* was one of the first aircraft carriers. It was a warship with a wooden deck added to it. It set sail in 1922. Soon, the U.S. Navy built new ships like the *Langley*. They carried fighter planes across the sea in **World War II**.

A plane prepares to land on the USS *Langley* in this photo.

CARRIERS TODAY

The U.S. Navy built new types, or classes, of aircraft carriers after World War II. The Enterprise class first set sail in 1961. The Nimitz class followed in 1975. These carriers can hold about 60 planes in their **hangars**.

Sailors bring planes from the hangar to the flight deck using big elevators.

The newest carriers in the U.S. Navy belong to the Ford class. These carriers can hold 75 or more aircraft in their hangars! They are larger, faster, and need fewer sailors than the older classes. They will serve the military for years to come.

USS *GERALD R. FORD* UNDER CONSTRUCTION

The USS *Gerald R. Ford*, shown here, was the first carrier of the Ford class. It's been in use since 2017.

WORDS TO KNOW

catapult: A machine for getting an airplane into the air at flying speed very quickly.

deliver: To take and hand over.

emergency: An unexpected situation that needs quick action.

hangar: An enclosed area where planes are kept and repaired.

military: Relating to the armed services.

pilot: Someone who flies a plane.

sailor: Someone who works on a boat or ship as part of the crew.

signal: A sign or action that sends a message.

tailhook: A hook on a plane used to catch cables to help it land on an aircraft carrier.

World War II: A war fought from 1939 to 1945 that involved countries around the world.

FOR MORE INFORMATION

BOOKS

Rajczak, Michael. *How an Aircraft Carrier Is Built.* New York, NY: Gareth Stevens Publishing, 2021.

Rogers, Marie. *Awesome Aircraft Carriers.* New York, NY: PowerKids Press, 2022.

WEBSITES

How Aircraft Carriers Work
https://science.howstuffworks.com/aircraft-carrier1.htm
Learn about the parts of an aircraft carrier with the descriptions and diagrams in this article.

U.S. Navy Aircraft Carriers
www.history.navy.mil/our-collections/photography/us-navy-ships/aircraft-carriers.html
Find images of aircraft carriers used by the U.S. Navy and facts about their history on this website.

INDEX